REVISIONING: MIRROR THERAPY

FOR UNRESOLVED GRIEF

MARK S. RIDER

Title ID: 4649663

ISBN-13 978-1495409462

NaturalPsychSolutions, Inc.
P.O. Box 1262
Grapevine, TX 76099

For Daphna, who swam in grief's unpredictable ocean

TABLE OF CONTENTS

INTRODUCTION   9

SECTION I: WHAT IS GRIEF

    THEORIES OF GRIEF   10

    THE PSYCHOPHYSIOLOGY OF GRIEF   15

    PERSISTENT COMPLEX
    BEREAVEMENT DISORDER   16

SECTION II: REVISIONING TECHNIQUE: MIRROR
THERAPY FOR UNRESOLVED GRIEF

    PHANTOM LIMB PAIN   21

    UNRESOLVED GRIEF AS "PHANTOM
    PERSON PAIN"   25

    REVISIONING PROCEDURE   28

    THREE STAGES OF REVISIONING   30

CASE STUDIES   33

SPECIFIC GUIDELINES FOR LEADING
A REVISIONING SESSION   48

SECTION III: THE NEUROLOGICAL BASIS FOR
PHANTOM PERSON PAIN

MIRROR NEURON NETWORK 54

THE DEFAULT MODE NETWORK 58

OTHER GRIEF NETWORKS   59

CLINICAL RESEARCH   63

MIRROR EXPOSURE   68

SUMMARY   73

REFERENCES   74

REVISIONING: MIRROR THERAPY

FOR

UNRESOLVED GRIEF

Relationships take up energy; letting go of them, psychiatrists theorize, entails mental work. When you lose someone you were close to, you have to reassess your picture of the world and your place in it. The more your identity was wrapped up with the deceased, the more difficult the loss.

— Meghan O'Rourke, poet, memoirist

INTRODUCTION

Grief is an experience which we all know personally. Every change in life - a death, the loss of a job, a divorce, a move, the process of aging, or even the infant being separated for a moment from its mother - evokes a grief reaction. This reaction may last for minutes or a lifetime, depending on the severity of the loss. Yet, the process of grieving is very similar for all of us. We may move from one stage to another in an extremely brief period of time, or get stuck in another stage for a lifetime.

Sometimes, psychotherapy can nudge us back into the process of grieving if we get stuck. Other times, the loss may take with it a part of our identity. This identity loss is one of the primary features that separate normal grief from what is now called in the DSM-V (2013), Persistent Complex Bereavement Disorder (PCBD). This concept will be discussed in detail in Section I, along with current theories of grief.

The main focus of this book, however, is to introduce the Revisioning technique as a major recovery tool for what will continue to be referred to in this book as "unresolved grief." PCBD unfortunately does not cover prolonged grief after divorce or estrangement, the victims of which can still have the same symptomatology. The technique is described in detail with case studies in Section II. Neurological research which led to the development of the Revisioning technique will also be covered.

In Section III, we will look at some of the brain networks and neurotransmitters hypothesized to be involved in Revisioning. Finally, some preliminary data on changes in these networks before and after Revisioning will be shared.

SECTION I

WHAT IS GRIEF

THEORIES OF GRIEF

Grief is the normal adaptation process to loss and change. It is a protective   mechanism that allows people to recover from major life changes. Nearly all cultures have grief rituals designed to remember and honor the deceased, and assist the mourners in moving on emotionally.

Freud was one of the first to address grief from a psychotherapeutic viewpoint (Freud, 1917). Central to his theory of repression, he believed that the "work of grief" was to resolve all the emotions connected to the departed person, not just those feelings present following the loss. Mourning was distinguished from melancholy (depression) as being a process whereby gradually, over time, less and less psychic energy (libido) was attached to the departed person, until the energy was liberated. Freud (1923) recognized that the withdrawal of the libido that attaches one person to another can take place only when the departed person has been "reinstated" within the ego. Although Freud conceptualized this process consuming months in psychoanalysis, the Revisioning process outlined in this book takes considerably less time. Like Freud, I have also found that one must first re-attach before one can detach, but due to a neurological mechanism instead.

Some research has challenged the long-standing belief in the necessity of "grief work" for adjustment to bereavement. No differences were found in depression between bereaved people who avoided confronting their loss and those who worked through their grief (Strobe, 1991). However, for widowers, participation in grief work was associated with better adjustment over an 18-month period.

From World War II on, grief experts tended to liken bereavement to the emotional experiences of a child who has separation anxiety from parents or toys

(Klein, 1940). Bowlby continued this line of thinking when he developed his "phases of grief", again based on the psychological responses to separation (1980). These phases include the following:

1. Shock and protest – numbness and disbelief

2. Preoccupation – yearning, searching and anger

3. Disorganization – despair

4. Resolution

Notice that these stages are reminiscent of Kubler-Ross's stages of death and dying (1969). Even though these stage models were developed on different populations ("mourners" for Bowlby and the "terminally ill" for Kubler-Ross), there are many consistencies between the two. Shock and denial mark the first stage, which unfortunately omits the implied term, fear.

Denial is the cover for fear. We wouldn't be in denial if we weren't afraid. Therefore, I call the first stage of any grieving process "fear." This is to punctuate the conceptualization of grief as a fluid movement through four *emotional* stages, fear, anger, sadness, and relief. I have given clients a rhyming scheme to easily understand emotions in general and the order with which they are experienced specifically in grief: Bad (fear), Mad, Sad, Glad, or Bad MSG (for those sensitive to sodium).

I often tell clients experiencing grief that *fear* is good because it communicates to others that you need support, or in the animal world, it conveys a need for protection from the herd. Shaking, trembling, teeth chattering, heart-pounding, freezing, and fleeing are all symptoms we have felt when afraid.

Anger, on the other hand, helps us overcome fear. In fact, social psychology research has demonstrated that those who expressed more anger than fear while participating in a stressful mental exercise had lower stress hormones than their counterparts (Lerner, 2005). Anger does appear to help empower us over fear. But anger can be toxic as well. There is a positive correlation between anger episodes and heart attacks. As a psychologist, I find that those stuck in the anger stage of grieving tend to have more negative outlooks, lower self-esteem, increased depression, and more relationship problems.

Sadness is the stage at which I find most people having reached the top of the grieving mountain. From here it is mostly downhill. Sadness, again like fear, communicates to others that we are in need of support. It is in this stage that I find that clients generally move on to acceptance and relief without much additional psychotherapeutic work. This is mostly true when other diagnoses are absent, *except* in the case of unresolved grief.

Another point to be made regarding grief is that it is experienced not just with negative life events, but positive ones as well. Holmes and Rahe (1967) brought this idea to fruition when they discovered that the top 24 life changes correlated with illness within six months contained many positive events (marriage, having a baby, and vacations) as well as negative ones (bankruptcy, jail time). That being said, the number one stressor was death of a spouse.

As a psychologist, I have seen people experience the various stages of grief to both negative and positive life events. In other words, the body has a universal mechanism to lessen the stress caused by loss and change; one that is independent of emotional valence. With every life change there is some kind of loss. The crying bride having the "wedding blues" may be happy about her new transition, but also grieving the loss of her bachelorette-hood.

THE PSYCHOPHYSIOLOGY OF GRIEF

One of the factors leading to one's being stuck in the grieving process is emotional repression. Freud's theory of repression is one of the few of his legacies that still underlies psychotherapy today (Freud, 1995).

Emotional repression has been found to predict mortality in those with coronary artery disease (Denollet, 2008). Emotional repression research has also found that the ache in your back may be the grief of several losses which have not been adequately resolved. In one study of emotional repression, people were subjected to painful stimuli (Burns et al., 2010). The emotional repressors reported more pain whereas the non-repressors reported more emotional distress. In other words, pain patients were found to have converted their emotional grief into physical pain.

Non-grievers (repressors) have additionally been discovered to have reduced activity in the parahippocampal gyrus in the brain. This tiny subcortical brain region has been found to have reduced size and activity in patients with major depression (Wang, 2013). However, teaching repressors how to express their feelings has been shown to cause the parahippocampal gyrus to light up again (de Greck, 2013).

More support for emotional grieving has been found in the content of emotionally-induced tears vs. those caused by exposure to a cut onion (Frey, 1983). The emotional tears had much higher concentrations of stress-induced proteins than in those elicited by onions. Weeping associated with grieving then is healthy because it reduces stress. Most of the patients I have seen in 25 years, become deeply relaxed after a brief cathartic cry. Tears can be counterproductive however, as seen in clinically-depressed people who weep, but often say they "don't know why they are crying."

More health benefits of crying were discovered when patients with colitis or ulcers were compared to healthy controls (Crepeau, 1981). Those with the stress-related disorders were more likely than the healthy people to "regard crying as a sign of weakness or loss of control." The patients also indicated that they cried less often in a variety of stressful situations.

PERSISTENT COMPLEX BEREAVEMENT DISORDER

According to the Center for Complicated Grief at Columbia University's School of Social Work (2013), "complicated grief is an intense and long-lasting form of grief that takes over a person's life." While a person may feel grief in some form for up to a lifetime after a person leaves, complicated grief refers to the emotional, cognitive, physical, and even spiritual dysfunction still prevalent after a period of at least six months.

Persistent Complex Bereavement Disorder (PCBD) is the new term for complicated or prolonged grief in the DSM-5. According to Prigerson, following the loss there is a period of separation distress accompanied by yearning and physical/emotional suffering as a result of the desired but unfulfilled reunion with the person. In my practice, a lot of people experience prolonged grief not only from death, but also through divorce or estrangement.

Other characteristics of PCBD include at least 5 of the following:

1. Feeling stunned, dazed or shocked (more than 6 months after the loss).

2. Feeling that a part of oneself has died.

3. Difficulty accepting the loss.

4. Avoidance of reminders of the reality of the loss.

5. Inability to trust others since the loss.

6. Bitterness or anger related to the loss.

7. Difficulty moving on with life.

8. Numbness (absence of emotion) since the loss.

9. Feeling that life is unfulfilling, empty, or meaningless since the loss.

Persistent Complex Bereavement Disorder is qualitatively different than bereavement-related depression (Prigerson, 1995). The symptoms listed above have shown more resistance to antidepressant medications, whereas the anxiety and depression subsequent to loss has been more successfully treated (Bui, 2012). Therefore, prolonged grief is more than a predisposition to depression or anxiety.

In the study of bereavement, attachment theory has been one of the most accepted. Attachment theory states that the bonds between loved ones are behaviorally conditioned. The conditioned stimulus is the loved one and the conditioned response is a reduction in distress and the generation of pleasure (O'Connor, 2012).

When a loved one has departed, there are two unrelated physiological components (Sbarra and Hazan, 2008). First, there is an "organized" stress response with the usual cascade of "fight or flight" responses including an increase in cortisol (immune suppressive), catecholamines (anxiety and depression), and heart rate and blood pressure (cardiovascular dysfunction).

The second component, the "disorganized" stress response is attachment-specific and originates from the loss of the rewarding aspects that the departed person represented. There is a loss of stress buffering due to the grieved person's absence and a loss of pleasure.

In one of the few studies comparing grief with complicated grief, cortisol was found to have a flatter diurnal rhythm in complicated grievers (O'Connor MF., Wellisch DK., Stanton AL., Olmstead R., Irwin, 2012). This study was important because it controlled for major depression, so the complicated grievers didn't have a lesser rhythm because of bereavement-related depression. This pattern of reduced cyclic variation in biological rhythms has been found in many medical disorders (Rider, 1997).

Reunion theory has also been proposed as a style of grieving (Bowlby, 1980). In contrast to attachment theory, reunion theory states that the person with complicated grief continues to struggle because the grief is a form of protest against the separation from the deceased, and serves to promote reunion with the lost person, not detachment. After the death, memories, photos, and other reminders continue to trigger yearning and grief. Learning to cope with these cues is a major task in adjusting to the death (Freed & Mann, 2007). If the detachment model is correct, then the perception of grief would be less and less rewarded over time with a reduction in dopamine's pleasure center in the nucleus acumbens of the brain. This is exactly what happened in the brains of grievers with non-complicated grief (O'Connor, et al., 2008). Reductions in activity of the nucleus acumbens (NA) was found in these folks over time. However, the complicated grievers experienced continued high activation of NA over time, giving some credence to reunion theory.

REVISIONING TECHNIQUE: MIRROR THERAPY

FOR

UNRESOLVED GRIEF

"You Must Re-attach To Detach"

PHANTOM LIMB PAIN

Revisioning is based on concepts and subsequent treatments for phantom limb pain that were introduced by V.S. Ramachandran (1998) fifteen years ago. A "phantom" is an unusual sensation, typically pain, that emanates from an amputated or disabled (as through stroke) limb. The pain is often felt as though the missing or dysfunctional limb were placed in an awkward or painful position. What Ramachandran discovered was that he could elicit the perception of touch in the amputated limb by moving a Q-tip along either the shoulder or the face on the same side as the missing limb. His patient could feel his lost hand being touched when stroking other parts of his body! The neurological cause of this phenomenon was quickly discovered due to the fMRI. Ramachandran's

Sensory-Motor Cortex cross-section showing amount of cortex relegated to body parts: Notice the hand and face take up most of the space; but when the hand is amputated, the face and shoulder move closer to each other (From Boucher, 2013).

research showed that the brain representation of the affected limb had receded after amputation, with the neighboring areas (the shoulder and face) "squatting" in the area formerly occupied by the hand. Demonstrating this brain plasticity was a remarkable thing in itself.

But even this neural squatting has its consequences in the form of phantom pain caused by the signals to and from the missing limb becoming out of phase. The phantom is due to perceptual mis-learning after the loss. Ramachandran (1998) calls this "learned paralysis." He also hypothesized that if the brain could redistribute itself following injury, then it could unlearn its faulty connections and reorganize to the original intact alignment.

He discovered the brilliant idea that by exposing the brain to the illusion of the limb *re-attached,* then one could unlearn this type of paralysis it was engaged in. Sometimes the simplest solution is the right one (Occam's razor). The mirror became the solution that many people suffering from phantom pain were looking for.

Conventional rehabilitation techniques were longer and slower to produce relief until mirror therapy was developed. As seen in the photograph of a mirror box, the right stump is placed in the box and by moving the fingers of the intact left hand, the illusion is created in the mirror that the right hand is re-

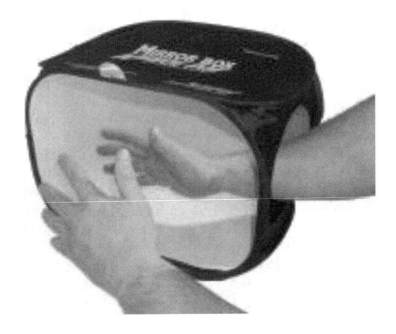

attached. Amputees using the mirror box actually feel their missing fingers moving again! Furthermore, the pain vanishes when the brain realigns the faulty connections.

By moving the good limb in the mirror, the mirror image looks anatomically correct and as if the missing limb were moving. This deception to the brain causes the previous sensations of discomfort and pain to disappear. Following mirror therapy, the cortical organization over the sensory-motor cortex has been found to return to normal, demonstrating remarkable brain plasticity (Michielsen, 2011).

In other words, the pain was real but not necessarily due to frayed nerve fibers near the amputation or injury. It was all in the brain! " The mirror allows the amputee to unlearn the paralysis and feel real (not phantom) movements. Patients were able to manipulate their amputated limbs out of uncomfortable positions, but only with the mirror.

UNRESOLVED GRIEF AS "PHANTOM PERSON PAIN"

To set out to prove this theory that unresolved grief involves a phantom person component, I began to use a type of therapy used in phantom limb pain recovery – mirror therapy . By using a mirror to simulate the movement of the disabled limb, the brain is "fooled" into believing the limb is functional again. It is hypothesized that in unresolved grief, the mourner's neurological representation of the departed person has also been redistributed, thus accounting for the unbearable psychological pain many people have.

In unresolved grief from traumatic loss, it is hypothesized that a neurological factor similar to phantom limb pain exists. Many people who are left behind say that in addition to the deep emotions felt, that "a part of them has been carved out", "that a piece of me is missing", and "I don't know who I am without them." This theory suggests that the person who departed left a cortical imprint in the brain of the bereaved.

However, trying to discover where our significant others are located in the brain is a little trickier. It is hypothesized in "phantom person pain" that there is a cognitive dissonance component in unresolved grief. When there is deep attachment to a person who has departed, a representation of the missing person is within the brain of the mourner. One likely source is the mirror neuron network (MNN), because in living with someone for a long time we learn to imitate many of their behaviors.

Another link to "where in the brain my beloved resides", is found in the ability of people's EEGs to entrain or synchronize. One study conducted healing sessions with an energy healer while EEGs were monitored in both recipients and healer (Hendricks, et al., 2010). During the healing sessions, many instances of frequency coupling of wave harmonics and instantaneous phase locking between the healer's and subjects' EEGs were documented. This entrainment occurred especially during alpha spindles recorded from the parietal cortex. The EEGs of the healer even entrained with the resonant frequency of the earth, 7.81 Hertz, also called the Schumann frequency.

Other examples of brainwave entrainment were found to occur in spatially separated individuals when recording from both EEGs (Wackerman, 2003; Radin, 2004; and Standish, 2004) and fMRI (Standish, 2003). This means that humans are not only connected mentally with other individuals, but that we carry the earth's resonant frequency in our brains too. Between-brain analyses have also provided evidence for neural resonance between individuals during social interactions (Schippers et al., 2010).

Some of the putative networks possibly involved in phantom person pain have been able to be elucidated due to fMRI. Because the subjects (reported in the EEG study above) were being influenced by a healer in the parietal cortical area, this area would seem to be important in keeping representations of a loved one. The parietal cortex, also called the secondary somato-sensory cortex, is in fact an important part of the mirror neuron network. The mirror neuron network is responsible for the phantom limb phenomena.

The deep loss is felt because the social-cognitive map of the mourned person is so deeply imprinted in the cortex that it's "amputation" leads to the equivalent of phantom limb pain. Just as in phantom limb syndrome, when the brain continues to send signals to the departed person but only gets jumbled feedback, then deep emotional pain results. The body maps that engage in the miscommunication with the phantom person are hypothesized to also be in the mirror neuron network of the brain.

One group of psychiatrists found that some of their patients with unresolved grief were found to have similar medical symptoms as their departed loved ones (Melson, 1982). Since these symptoms were medically unsubstantiated, it appears that the empathy and imitation generated by the mirror neuron network of one's dearly departed has continued to stir up realistic, sympathetic, painful memories. In many of these cases needless medical and surgical procedures were performed.

This implies that the mirror neuron network is involved in unresolved grief. Through the processes of empathy and imitation unique to the mirror neuron network, symptoms are learned from the departed one and retained in the mourner. It might be that the mirror neuron network is dysfunctional in the longing and yearning phases of grief.

REVISIONING PROCEDURE

In Revisioning, the mourned person is reunited with the bereaved on a couch or using two armless chairs side-by-side. This process is much different than looking at photographs. Most people with unresolved grief have pictures of their lost loved ones that they see daily in their homes. Yet, their grief remains. In fact, many say that pictures of their loved ones often stirs up the grief rather than helping with it.

In Revisioning I use two thin boards (one 3' X 1" and the other 2" X 1") attached perpendicularly in the shape of a cross. A turtleneck sweater is mounted over the cross and it is propped upright on the couch next to the client. The mourned person's life-sized "head shot" picture is taped to the top of the vertical board and finally, denim pants are placed on the couch simulating the legs. A mirror (at least 20 inches wide) is placed in front of them so the client can see themselves next to the departed person. The client is told to watch their reflection for 10 minutes, feeling free to comment on their perceptions, feelings, and thoughts.

I have found that making occasional reflective comments helps the client talk about their experience. There was a need to do more questioning at first to attempt to discern what they were going through. Fortunately, this did not interfere with the process and added valuable information about the process they were experiencing.

Results from clinical use of Revisioning have been to create a dramatic emotional release in clients subsiding rapidly in intensity over a 10-minute period. If repeated several more times on subsequent days or weeks, the effect is far less emotional. Most clients have not required more than one session because the effect is so strong and lasting. This observation appears to confirm the neurological basis to Revisioning. Normal grief reactions and catharses are impactful but may not address the cognitive dissonance element seen in unresolved grief. One can see this happening relatively quickly as the client makes the body gesture of a "double take," shaking their head and blinking their eyes.

Sometimes clients feel tension or frustration at first if the parting by the mourned one resulted in a lot of anger. Once the cognitive dissonance element resolves and the patient settles into the procedure, the feeling stages of grief outlined by Kubler-Ross (1969) proceed without any obstacles. One can observe anger leading to sadness and then to acceptance, all within a 10-minute period. Many times, medically treated depression has resolved completely.

THREE STAGES OF REVISIONING

There are three stages which clients tend to experience during the Revisioning technique. These are, in order:

> 1. Cognitive Dissonance stage (or Re-Attachment) — a mental sensation of something "weird" or "not quite right", in seeing the departed person suddenly next to them on the couch

2. Cathartic stage - physical tension or restlessness followed by cathartic release (anger, weeping, etc.)

3. Reintegration stage - marked by physical relaxation and reduced emotional expression

As we shall see in Section III, the pre-Cathartic condition is related to hyper-functioning of the default mode network, the idling network of the brain. In cases of traumatic loss and depression, the default mode network (DMN) has been found to operate like a car in park with the accelerator pushed to the floor. And just as the car in this condition is needlessly burning its own fuel, our bodies are wasting its own needed fuel and causing unnecessary wear and tear during traumatic loss and unresolved grief.

It is hypothesized that before the Cathartic stage can occur, the Cognitive Dissonance stage must resolve. The brain must reintegrate the loss perceptually before the procession of feelings can occur. This catharsis then takes the metaphorical foot off the accelerator and reduces the hyper-functioning of the DMN. Preliminary evidence has indicated that the DMN was deactivated, as defined by reduced EEG activity over the prefrontal cortex, following the Revisioning technique (see Clinical Research).

During the Cognitive Dissonance stage, the mirror neuron network (MNN) is hypothesized to increase its activity. In fMRI studies, mirror therapy has produced a shift in brain activity over the sensory-motor cortex of the affected cortical area (Michielsen, 2011). This network is activated during the behaviors of imitation and empathy. As one would expect, it is hard to engage in imitation and empathy when one's mind is spinning with loss, anxiety, and depression. Therefore the DMN and the MNN appear to be complementary and their behavior is negatively correlated.

In the Reintegration stage, it is hypothesized that the brain signals to and from the phantom person come into phase and this correction allows the person to feel relaxed and have the sense of completion of the grief process.

Revisioning therefore involves a dynamic interplay between at least the DMN and MNN and possibly other networks as well. If the mirror neuron network becomes dysfunctional due do misrepresentations in the brain, then the default mode network goes into high gear, much like my old laptop when it starts running scripts and sounds like it is going to liftoff! I can reset my laptop by turning it off, but mirror therapy may be the only tool to reset the brain during unresolved grief and provide relief.

CASE STUDIES

Case Study 1

This female client was suddenly abandoned by her partner after a presumably happy 23 year marriage; traditional supportive counseling, EMDR, cognitive therapy, meditation, and antidepressant medication minimally affected symptoms of depression and anxiety after 10 months of treatment. Session 1 of Revisioning was embarked upon with her remarking how weird it was to be sitting next to him. This is an example of the Cognitive Dissonance stage, in which the client begins the psychological re-attachment with the departed person with its proposed neurological reorganization within the mirror neuron network.

This was quickly followed by a cathartic mix of anger and then sadness. She was restless and uncomfortable for the first five minutes seeing the two of them together on the couch (in the mirror). The next five minutes resulted in less restlessness but still a lot of crying. The reduced motor restlessness is seen as a reduction in the default mode network.

On day 2 the client repeated the procedure at home for ten minutes. She reported feeling much more relaxed this time and felt sad but didn't cry. I saw her again on day 4 with her reporting that she had repeated the procedure on day 3 with only relaxation. She said her depression had completely lifted. I saw her again one week later, and without repeating the Revisioning any further, her depression still abated.

Within two weeks of the Revisioning she was able to talk with her ex about issues related to their divorce and kids without crying. Some anxiety persisted two months after the Revisioning due to uncertainties in her new life, but the depression never returned.

Case Study 2

This adult male was abandoned by his mother in emotional and physical ways growing up and finally through death when the client was 45. Years of therapy had revealed stubbornness to trust and an emotional wall that left him feeling alone, anxious, and depressed. His Revisioning session resulted in considerable distress initially. He moved his shoulders away from his mother before Revisioning, an attempt to distance himself from her. This represents the Cognitive Dissonance stage. He said he felt angry as a child when his rather obese mom would try to hug him.

However, when Revisioning started, he began to almost lean-in to his mom. Toward the end of the ten minutes, the client relaxed his body more and started to tear up. Here Cognitive Dissonance leads to the Cathartic stage. After a break to discuss his feelings, we repeated the Revisioning, this time having his mom lie down in his lap. He relaxed and cried some more.

One month follow-up indicated that he had not repeated the procedure but felt a significant shift in his attitudes about his mother and a general improvement in depression. She had become Reintegrated back into his mental schema.

Case Study 3

This woman lost an adult child to chronic gastric disease. She had battled with depression and guilt since his death 7 years ago. Even her relationships with her remaining children became strained. Therapeutically, she had completed two years of psychotherapy, including many EMDR sessions. She was also taking antidepressant medication and yet this loss still had a major grip on her. Doing the Revisioning with her the first time was emotional and cathartic. She remembered the last good day she had with him before he died. A week later she remarked that her thoughts about her son had dropped off significantly with less depression and guilt. (I have found that no parent who loses a child does not feel guilt). Months later, she truly felt she was moving on from her son's death.

Case Study 4

A male patient remarked during the initial interview that he had not been able to move on from his dad's death five years earlier. After being asked if he wanted to try something to bring more closure to his loss, he consented.

During the Revisioning, he very quickly became tense and his vision blurred. I told him to breathe to allow the emotions to come out. He began to cry softly. After about five minutes, his physical demeanor relaxed significantly. After ten minutes total, he remarked that he felt much calmer and not sad anymore.

Follow-up one week later revealed that he had experienced less thoughts of yearning and longing for his dad than before the Revisioning. Feeling that he had made considerable progress, a decision was made not to repeat the Revisioning. Two-month follow-up found that he still had no intrusive thoughts or feelings about his father.

Case Study 5

This young woman was still grieving over her divorce 5 years prior. She reported feeling "unable to move on, stuck, and that a piece of her had been removed after her divorce." I asked her what it was like sitting next to her ex on the couch. She said "it is weird but kind of completing; so much of me was tied up in him." The Cognitive Dissonance stage was traversed quickly as her tension led to crying. After about eight minutes in the Catharsis stage, she began to relax. After the ten minutes, she continued to feel relaxed. I asked her if she still felt sad or depressed and she said "it is what it is," without any hint of sadness or anger. It were as if she felt truly centered and calm.

One week follow-up revealed that she had not thought of her ex on a daily basis as she had before the Revisioning. She had even gone out on a date, which was something she had not thought of doing in a long time. Communication with her ex regarding their kids also became easier. At two-month follow-up she was in a committed relationship and experiencing a new independence and sense of identity separate from her ex.

Case Study 6

This male client was suffering from a long history of childhood physical abuse by his father which was enabled by his mom. He still felt a lot of anger toward her, even after months of counseling consisting of EMDR, emotional support, cognitive therapy, and medication.

The Revisioning was done because there had been long periods of estrangement where he had been too angry to have a relationship with her. Upon seeing her reflection next to his on the couch, he began to converse with her about feelings he had not been able to verbalize directly to her, due to her defensiveness.

Again, after five minutes, he relaxed and felt like he had nothing left to say to her. Upon reaching ten minutes, the session ended and he felt calmer. At two-month follow-up, he was far less depressed and indicated that he was having fewer intrusive thoughts about his mother.

Case Study 7

This client had unresolved grief stemming from her grandson's suicide six years prior. EMDR was used early in treatment for the traumatic nature of her loss. She also took antidepressant medication. She had been very close to him and was also feeing guilt because she was one of the last people to hear from him before his death. She still felt intense longing for him and that a part of herself went with him.

During the onset of Revisioning, she remarked how "unusual" it felt to see him sitting with her. The Cognitive Dissonance stage lasted very briefly however as she then became tense and expressed anger for him taking his own life. Her Cathartic stage became quite fluid as her anger was replaced by tears. She wept for several minutes as she mused, "I don't know why I didn't see anything coming, I just saw him the day before."

After another couple of minutes her tone shifted again to one of acceptance as she smiled, "how can you be mad at that goofy face." Then she added, "no one could make me smile like him." As she wept, she could feel less tension in her chest and her body movements diminished.

Shortly thereafter, she became completely calm and had no further shifts in sensations, thoughts, or feelings. Reintegration had now been accomplished. At the two-week follow-up she said that she had less intrusive thoughts about him and the psychomotor retardation of her depression had lifted. Two-month follow-up found that she was still depression-free and had returned to work with additional energy.

Case Study 8

This female had been divorced for 10 years and complained that after her husband left, she still felt unworthy and unattractive. She thought he had been her soulmate and his departure had created a "hole inside, like something had been removed." This was representative of the Cognitive Dissonance stage. She had an especially wonderful physical relationship with him. In rejecting thoughts of him since their divorce, she began to neglect, or reject, parts of her body that reminded her of closeness to him. The theory being proposed here is that body neglect can cause physical issues such as pain because the cortical representations of these neglected body areas reorganize, just as in phantom limb pain. She had developed severe abdominal pain since he had left 10 years ago.

Revisioning immediately triggered a release of anger as she said "looking at him with me makes my stomach turn and my head feels like exploding." This is an example of the phantom person pain described earlier. Continuing to look at the two of them in the mirror, she began to reduce her nearly hyperactive restlessness after about 5 minutes. Her abdominal pain subsided as well. Physical pain can abruptly disappear when the cognitive dissonance is resolved through re-attachment. She calmed but then said she felt lousy because it brought back the old idea of reconciling with him." She relaxed even further and felt no additional shifts in perceptions, thoughts, or feelings.

A week later we decided to revisit the Revisioning because it didn't seem that she had completed the cathartic stage, and therefore may not have reintegrated. This time she noticed how tense her muscles were and that she was able to relax her body. She relaxed very quickly and said she no longer felt anger or sadness, only pity. She felt more completed this time. It appears that although one Revisioning session may suffice for some people, the rule of thumb may be to continue to do 10-minute

Revisioning sessions until there are no additional shifts in perceptions, thoughts, or feelings.

Case Study 9

This client lost her mother to drug addiction eight years ago. Her mother had never known my client's husband or kids. She felt like there was a part missing when she died because she had just been starting to foster a relationship with her after years of estrangement when she overdosed. "We were finally for the first time in our lives beginning to enjoy each other."

The Revisioning started with sadness and disappointment because the dreams of reconnecting with her had been crushed. Motor restlessness was evident during the cognitive dissonance stage. In general, the cognitive dissonance stage appears to be accompanied by a dramatic increase in limb movements, possibly due to increased mirror neuron activity. This phenomenon parallels the broken image the mourner has of their relationship. It is hypothesized that the Revisioning of themselves reunited with their partner mends this broken image, which is then followed by a reduction in restlessness and a greater sense of completeness. Again, Revisioning adds the neuro-cognitive element to the repair of grief, leading to more complete reintegration.

Following the ten minute Revisioning she felt calmer, with more of a sense of completeness. A little humor overcame her as she smiled, "look at her, why did she get all the hair and good looks." At two-month follow-up, she was having fewer bouts of sadness and anger with less thoughts in general about her mother.

Case Study 10

This woman lost her mother two years ago to cancer, which was diagnosed within just weeks of her death. She commented at the beginning of the Revisioning session that she still missed her mom now as much as when she died. She sobbed, "I lost my center when mom died; she was my "everything is going to be OK" voice."

At the beginning of Revisioning, I asked what it was like to see her mom sitting next to her on the couch. She replied, "this is the way it is supposed to be." The cognitive dissonance stage resolved into the cathartic stage as she began to weep. After five minutes she was still tearful but starting to feel calmer. After three more minutes she stopped sobbing and said she felt "strangely relaxed." No more feelings arose and she appeared to have reintegrated her mom back into her cognitive schema.

Follow-up found her reporting that she could now talk about her mother without crying. Another result was that her attitude with her sisters showed improvement.

Case Study 11

This married woman had entered counseling for depression and self-esteem issues. She was estranged from an abusive father except for a couple of hours at a time every few years or so. It was clear that the abuse had contributed significantly to both issues of concern. Cognitive therapy and EMDR had been used for months with modest improvements. Medications were also being taken.

Revisioning was approached gently for I had not attempted this technique with an estranged parent who was also the perpetrator of abuse. She was willing to attempt the procedure, after all, "it was only his picture."

The Cognitive Dissonance stage was witnessed as she found it hard to look at him. "Its bad enough that I look like him." Then, she realized, "I spent so much time resenting him that I resented myself." Her body image had taken a hit probably out of cortical neglect. In rejecting her father, she had also neglected the cortical areas corresponding to her body. In addition to experiencing a poor body image, she was also dealing with pain in various parts of her body.

Tension increased and she became restless. Anger began to appear as she said, "neither of us deal with anger well." Within a couple of minutes, she began to weep as she questioned, "what is my responsibility to him now." The cathartic stage lasted a few more minutes as she began to resolve her feelings of grief and reintegrate him back into her mental schema.

One month following the Revisioning procedure has found that this patient increased her self-esteem by four points on a 1-10 rating scale, whereas cognitive therapy alone increased self-esteem by only two points over the one year period preceding that.

Case Study 12

This young woman was living in this country while her mother was going through rapid deterioration with Alzheimer's disease in another country. She felt helpless that she couldn't be there to help, and guilt that her brother and father were handling everything. She could only return home once a year due to her job. She had entered counseling because of symptoms of depression and anxiety.

Revisioning was done to help with her anxiety about her mother's condition and her inability to help out. She immediately remarked how weird this was to see the two of them together (Cognitive Dissonance stage). "This is like I'm reviving her, it's shooting me back through all my life with her." What the re-attachment provided however, was a mental schema of support from her mom that she hadn't had in years due to the absence and her mother's illness.

The Cathartic stage was entered within 1-2 minutes of the start. While most of the memories she had were positive, there was lots of sadness as she wept through the next few minutes. "What's coming up now is stuff I can't talk to her about anymore." Then she began to explain how her mother would normally tell her "not to worry" (about a sensitive issue that had come up with my client's husband); "you won't experience as much emotional pain as you think you will."

Here, the reattachment with her mother is a mirror neuron behavior. She is recanting her mother's thoughts through imitation, what she's heard her mother say before. This process was manifested very quickly through the use of the mirror.

By the end of the ten-minute Revisioning procedure, she calmed significantly and stopped weeping. She had reintegrated her mother back into her brain as a form of support she still uses to this day. At two-month follow-up she was sad but not having depression or loss of identity even though her mother was continuing to deteriorate.

Case Study 13

This client entered counseling to discover why she kept having self-destructive relationships. Physical abusiveness was reported to have occurred in a previous marriage for 10 years. Cognitive Therapy produced mild results for negative self-esteem issues.

Because of the traumatic nature of her marriage, we then attempted Eye Movement Desensitization and Reprocessing (EMDR) to repair the emotional and mental damage possibly blocking her Cognitive Therapy from working. Upon commencement of the EMDR procedure, she reported difficulty in vividly remembering any of the traumatic events. She reported that she couldn't feel any emotions associated with the traumas either.

A consideration was made that the Revisioning procedure would be too aversive for her to attempt; she didn't need to see her attacker seated next to her on the couch. However, the power of this technique is so unique that I made an adjustment just to help her unlock some of her emotions. I asked her to "*imagine that the back of the chair in front you is a mirror; and in this imaginary mirror I want you to see your ex sitting on the couch next to you.*" This imaginary Revisioning exercise provided the key to unlock her feelings as they cascaded out.

Following the cathartic stage we immediately returned to the uncompleted EMDR session to finally desensitize the traumas and reprocess her self-esteem in relationship to these traumas. With her cognitive repair, she since has learned to set better boundaries and integrate a more positive self-esteem into her relationship schema.

Case Study 14

A young married woman's mother had run off when the patient was 12. During this estrangement, she had no support and had to put her mom in the recesses of her mind and heart. Revisioning started with a lot of body movements that she reported as nervousness. Then, she started to weep and said she was "angry that she put me in this position." "I was so dependent on her as a child, I stuck to her like Velcro."

As she came to the end of the Cathartic stage, she started to relax and remember some positive memories. "She was very smart and could do anything, and very funny." She then began to employ some empathy (mirror neuron behavior) as she remarked, "I can understand some of what she went through."

After one month, she was far less depressed and as a result of her increase in self-esteem (increased by 3 points on a 1-10 rating scale after the Revisioning alone) was becoming more assertive and even expressed anger for the first time in years. Anger was an emotion that had lost its voice and perhaps its cortical representation in the brain following her mother's sudden departure. Revisioning had given it back to her. But, Revisioning had also taken away her abandonment-related depression, which was still in remission two months later.

Case Study 15

This middle-aged male had been estranged from his father since their divorce when he was a child. At the beginning of Revisioning, he felt Cognitive Dissonance as he did a double-take and remarked, "this is weird seeing him next to me." He then quickly entered the Cathartic stage with a mixture of anger and sadness. "I am thinking of all the things we used to do together." "But I'm mad at him for not being honest, and if I saw him I think I would hit him."

As he became more Reintegrated, he offered, "Gosh, he looks so young, and when he was around he was a good dad and played with us." Two-week follow-up found that he was much less angry with his father. He also experienced less yearning and longing for his dad. Even pictures of his dad evoked far less sadness than they had two weeks before.

SPECIFIC GUIDELINES FOR LEADING A REVISIONING SESSION

Specific guidelines are proposed for the utilization of the Revisioning experience. These are intended as a format incorporating the philosophy of "do no harm." Revisioning is an experimental technique that is powerful and therefore must be proceeded with caution as to the many possibilities of experiences.

Motivation

Some clients may not be motivated in grieving or "getting over" the loss of a loved one. They may fear or feel guilty about "forgetting" their loved one. With grief, however, it seems that patients lose motivation more due to inertia than anything else. These patients have tried every other treatment to lessen their depression, anxiety, and loss of identity, but many times with only modest gains. The grief sometimes takes a life of its own and the sufferer tries valiantly to make new sense of the world but cannot successfully lift off. This may account for the statistics showing that mourners have a higher mortality rate in the first year following death of a spouse.

Therefore, like most treatments, the client should always be informed as to the nature of the treatment and their consent be obtained.

Guidance

Guidance by a licensed professional with some experience in leading a Revisioning session is highly recommended. The research on guided Revisioning sessions conducted so far has been highly successful in decreasing unresolved grief (95% for those with PCBD). Therapeutic guidance is not only important for outcome, but can help the client not get stuck in any of the stages. Some clients tend to drift in their attention and forget to look at the mirror, so guiding them back to the mirror can be helpful.

The amount of talking by clients can be large or small. As long as their focus is on describing memories, discussing their relationship, emoting, etc., then the client probably does not have to be prompted. If a minute has gone by without a word, then I will usually ask them, "have you experienced any changes in thoughts, feelings, or perceptions?"

Most of the different thoughts and feelings have been expressed within about ten minutes. Toward the end, the client usually reduces dramatically the restless body movements and reports relaxation. If it appears that they made some progress in expressing different emotions, but didn't get to the relaxation inherent in the Reintegration stage, they will probably benefit from repeating the exercise with or without therapeutic guidance.

Populations

There may be some populations of clients that may not be suited for Revisioning. I have conducted successful sessions with patients with severe depression and severe but medically controlled bipolar disorder. Before conducting sessions with clients representing these two populations, suicidality should be assessed and considered in the context of a potentially profound and cathartic experience like Revisioning. The calming effects seen in all participants thus far after the 10-minute procedure does not necessarily mean that everyone will have this experience. Consult with DrMarkRider.com/Revisioning for further updates on this procedure.

Clients with trauma and PTSD have also participated in Revisioning sessions with success. However, many times, the person whose death, divorce, or estrangement that the client is still grieving may have also been responsible for abuse or neglect to the client. This is obviously a complex situation and many factors must be considered.

In some cases, the clients' fear and anger have been so great that Revisioning was not attempted in favor of a trauma-resolution technique like Eye Movement Desensitization and Reprocessing (EMDR). Whereas EMDR can be successful in desensitizing the client to anxiety and Cognitive Therapy effective in treating the depression, the unresolved grief involving these losses still often remains as a therapeutic hurdle.

Revisioning was attempted successfully with two individuals involving childhood trauma (Case Studies 6, and 11). In both cases, the abusers/neglecters were parents with whom the clients still had some form of a relationship. The clients' willingness to participate in the procedure was probably due to the fact that the parents were still involved with them in at least some capacity.

In another client (Case Study 13) who was divorced and estranged from a past abusive marriage, EMDR and Cognitive Therapy were attempted to interrupt the damage to her self esteem which still pervaded her relationships since their divorce. I had not considered Revisioning due to the severity of the trauma and her revulsion of him. However, the EMDR was at first unsuccessful due to her dissociation from the frightening memories. She simply could not or would not let the memories and associated feelings emerge. At this point, I did a modification of the Revisioning in which I instructed her to look at the back of a chair I placed in front of her. I then asked her if she could imagine a mirror hanging on the back of the chair. And in that mirror she could see her ex sitting next to her on the couch. Immediately, she began to get angry and then cry. After a few minutes, the EMDR was then reattempted successfully as the memories that unfolded had feelings attached to them, which could then be desensitized with Cognitive Therapy.

Timing

The definition for the temporal aspects of loss when it becomes traumatic (PTSD) or "persistently complex" are both found in the DSM-V to be six months following the loss. This means that the diagnoses of PTSD and Complex Bereavement can't be substantiated for at least six months.

Nevertheless, just like EMDR for trauma resolution, Revisioning can be conducted at any time following the loss. Doing it early following a loss can prevent the loss from becoming unresolved or complicated.

THE NEUROLOGICAL BASIS FOR PHANTOM PERSON PAIN

In this Section, the case will be made that persistent, complex bereavement has a mirror neuron component that is faulty in filling in the loss of identity that most of these folks have. Since no studies of the mirror neuron network have been made during grief, we will have to start with conditions like depression that are experienced during bereavement.

MIRROR NEURON NETWORK

First, the mirror neuron network (MNN) has been found to be activated during several activities, which I refer to as the 3 M's:

1. eMpathy

2. iMitation

3. iMagination

Mirror neurons have been dubbed "empathy neurons" because they become activated when we put ourselves in others' shoes. They are also the motor neurons that become active when we are imitating or imagining imitating something (just observing another's actions can activate the MNN). Mirror neurons are found in the sensory-motor cortex as described in Section II, as well as the adjacent parts of the frontal, parietal, and temporal lobes.

People with depression have been found to have more limited abilities to empathize (Schreiter, 2013), suggesting mirror neuron dysfunction. Imagination, another of the three M's of the mirror neuron system, has also been found to be more difficult when depressed (Cocude, 1997). Imitation abilities and empathy abilities activated the mirror neuron system to a lower degree in young moms experiencing postpartum depression than in healthy controls (Ammaniti, unpublished report).

In autism, there is commonly found a lack of empathy in addition to a dysfunctional mirror neuron network. A commonly used protocol to assess mirror neuron activity is to record EEG over the sensory-motor cortex and observe mu (8-12 Hz) brainwave suppression when subjects are observing others perform actions (Oberman et al., 2005). The mu brainwave suppression will occur to imitated actions (such as grasping a pen) but not to observed actions when the MNN is dysfunctional. Children with Autism Spectrum Disorders (ASD) have been found to have a dysfunctional MNN in this way.

One of the primary brain chemicals associated with the mirror neuron network is oxytocin, the "empathy" neuropeptide associated with bonding and prosocial behaviors. In a meta-analysis of studies on the effects of nasally administered oxytocin on the treatment of different clinical groups, only the Autism Spectrum Disorders (ASD) were found to benefit (Bakermans-Kranenburg and Jzendoorn, 2013). The likely mechanism here being that oxytocin can improve the functioning of a faulty mirror neuron network.

In fact these very results occurred in a study of the effect of oxytocin on the mirror neuron network. EEG mu suppression was significantly increased in subjects who had inhaled oxytocin vs. placebo while observing a person walking (Perry, 2010).

Anorectics have also been found to have deficits in the mirror neuron network. Therefore, mirror exposure (see Mirror Exposure section) may work by activating the MNN in those with eating disorders. Oxytocin production is also reduced in anorectics. As we recall from earlier in this Section, autism spectrum individuals have a dysfunctional mirror neuron network and reduced oxytocin levels. While some have compared autism to anorexia (Huke et al., 2013), the fact remains that by activating the mirror neuron network and consequent increase in oxytocin, potential therapies can be developed for those with autism and anorexia.

Many times, the person experiencing grief has not only lost a loved one, but also a major source of empathy and comfort during such stressful times. Hence, this becomes a double loss. Oxytocin studies have not been conducted in grievers, but levels of this neuropeptide might fall significantly after a loss, just as they do in women with post-partum depression (Skruntz, 2011).

Revisioning activates the mirror neuron network because when one sees one's reflection in the mirror, the mourner is usually moving and adjusting on the couch. There is usually more cognitive and emotional tension during the first 5 minutes of the Revisioning technique. The hypothesis here is that the dysfunctional MNN in prolonged grievers is accompanied by lowered oxytocin levels, which have been associated with higher levels of anxiety (Nissen et al., 1998). Therefore, the reduction in motor restlessness following Revisioning is probably related to the higher oxytocin produced during the procedure.

In addition, the motor map of the departed person is repaired within the mourner due to this "active" reunion on the couch. This is perhaps why looking at pictures of the departed, a passive process not involving the mirror neuron network, does not give as much therapeutic aid to grieving people, and can even exacerbate the process in unresolved grief. Revisioning allows them to activate the mirror neuron network and possibly increase oxytocin levels and further prosocial behaviors.

THE DEFAULT MODE NETWORK

In addition to the mirror neuron network (MNN), the default mode network (DMN) is also involved in the grief response. But unlike the MNN, which as we have seen, was disrupted and probably under-functioning in unresolved grief, the DMN is overactive during mourning. Whether these two systems are negatively correlated with each other remains to be seen. Nevertheless, the MNN and DMN are dynamically related (Molnar-Szakacs and Uddin, 2013).

If one's place or identity in the world has been seriously disrupted, such as through unresolved grief, then the default mode network will be affected. The DMN includes the medial prefrontal cortex, the medial temporal lobe, the posterior cingulate cortex, precuneus and the medial, lateral and inferior parietal cortex.

Preston and de Waal (2002), in their theory of emotional-motor resonance, see the MNN as a lower level of empathy called "embodied simulation." Embodied simulation is the process of transforming perceived actions and emotions into our own inner representations of those actions and emotions. On the other hand, the DMN involves higher levels of empathy called "mentalizing" (rather than "simulating"), which is the process of understanding another person's view. During unresolved grief, the dynamic balance between these networks has been tilted.

In bereaved patients, words that triggered thoughts of grief lit up the prefrontal cortex (part of the DMN) and the adjacent amygdala (Freed, Yanagihara, Hirsch, and Mann, 2009). The DMN is called "default" because it is like the idling gear of the brain. However, during grief, depression (Sambataro, et al., 2013), trauma (Landin-Romero et al., 2013), and narcissism (Jankowiak-Siuda, Zajkowski, 2013), the activity of the DMN is similar to putting your car in park and revving the engine. It has been suggested that the ruminations that accompany grief, depression, and trauma are caused by the functional hyperactivity of the DMN (Brzezicka, 2013).

OTHER GRIEF NETWORKS

Pain Network

As mentioned in Section I, under the discussion of the detachment and reunion theories of grief, the pain activation network was stimulated when mourners were exposed to pictures or words referencing their loss (O'Connor, 2008). The three regions linked to pain processes are the anterior cingulate cortex (ACC), the insula, and the periaqueductal gray area. Although the comparisons were not significant, there was a trend for the complicated grievers to show less activation in these pain areas than the uncomplicated grievers. Activation of these pain areas (fMRI) however has been determined to be inverse to the level of pain felt (LaCesa, 2013). This means that the pain areas of the brain are activated during grief and that complicated grievers experience more pain than non-complicated grievers.

Dopamine Reward Network

In the O'Connor study mentioned above, one other area in the brain that differentiated complicated from non-complicated grievers was the nucleus accumbens (NA), the primary dopamine reward center of the brain. Activity in the NA was also associated with more longing and yearning for the deceased. In normal grief, the NA activation is highest when the loss is first experienced and declines as the grief is resolved. However, in prolonged grief the NA activation appears to stay elevated without receding.

The likely scenario is that the dopamine reserves are low in people who experience unresolved grief. Consequently, the increased activation of the NA in prolonged grief is because the NA is struggling to produce more dopamine but can't. The dopamine system has also been found to run parallel to the oxytocin system (Baskerville, 2010). This makes logical sense in the case of grief because we are currently postulating that the oxytocin system is dysfunctional in unresolved grief along with the mirror neuron network.

Immune System

Grief attacks the immune system also. Pro-inflammatory cytokines (interleukin-1β and soluble tumor necrosis factor receptor II) were elevated in women suffering bereavement (O'Connor, 2009). These immune factors increase autoimmune diseases such as rheumatoid arthritis and irritable bowel syndrome. Brain activity in the pre-frontal cortex (part of the DMN) was also increased by the stress of bereavement.

Decreased oxytocin has been found to be linked to cytokine production (Norman, 2010). Therefore, when prolonged grief strikes, the mirror neuron network probably becomes compromised leading to reduced oxytocin levels and consequent immune hyperactivity and autoimmune illness.

Nonlinear Dynamics of Grief

Individuals with persistent complex bereavement disorder have been found to exhibit increased stress levels over those experiencing normal grief reactions. Stress was measured using circadian cortisol variations. Cortisol is the body's stress hormone and is immunosuppressive. The cortisol rhythm in prolonged mourners was flatter than in the non-prolonged mourners (O'Connor et al., 2009). This reduced variation in daily cortisol rhythms was also found in stressed-out, shift-working nurses in a pervious study by this author (Rider, 1985), and has been found to be correlated with lower cancer survival (Sephton et al., 2013). Having less cyclic rhythmicity in biological cycles, such as heart rate, has lead to higher incidence of heart attacks (Kleiger et al., 1990). Less cyclic variation in different EEG brainwaves has been correlated with immune disorders (Rider, 1997). Quasi-periodic variation has been called nonlinear behavior or complexity in science. Reduced complexity in all biological rhythms has been correlated with increased illness.

Because grief now has been found to activate several brain networks, the interaction of these networks creates nonlinear dynamics and increased complexity. Grief itself has been found to exhibit cyclic variation in reported emotional well-being during bereavement (Bisconti, et al., 2006). A circaseptan (near-weekly) rhythm was found in this research. This may be because circaseptan rhythms have also been found in mood research, with positive mood demonstrating a predominant circadian (daily) rhythm while negative mood has more circaseptan variation (Cornelissen, 2005).

Measuring grief symptoms since the death of a loved one has differentiated three patterns of grievers (Bonanno, 2004). Different temporal courses of grief have been found to characterize these types of grievers. In the Resilient and Recovery Types, there were more accelerated improvements at first followed by a more gradual slope until no symptoms were experienced. This type of recovery pattern is indicative of the nonlinear dynamics found in healthy individuals. The Chronic Grief Type, however, showed no dynamics, just perpetually high grief symptoms over a period of years. This reduced nonlinear pattern possibly indicated that one of the brain networks involved in prolonged grief recovery is dysfunctional. It is hypothesized here that the mirror neuron network is precisely that faulty system.

A similar temporal pattern to recovery was documented in subjects in measuring the degree of forgiveness following a transgression by a friend (McCullough, 2010). Subjects' level of forgiveness was significantly faster in the first half of the time it took to completely forgive, than in the second half of time. This nonlinear pattern of forgiving is very similar to that of grieving and would therefore appear to involve some of the same brain networks.

CLINICAL RESEARCH

Research was conducted on the Revisioning procedure to see if the benefits could be quantified in terms of measurable outcomes. Secondly, some of the clients were willing to undergo EEG monitoring during the procedure so that mirror neuron and default mode activity could be assessed. No research has thus far been conducted on mirror neuron activity before and after any interventions with such a short time interval (10 minutes).

Clinical research on Revisioning has consisted of four test instruments:

> The Inventory of Complicated Grief (Prigerson et al., 1995)
>
> The Basic Empathy Scale (Jolliffe, Farrington, 2006)
>
> The Vividness of Visual Imagery Questionnaire (Marks, 1973)
>
> EEG pre- and post-test data on 5 clients. Mu suppression was measured with an active electrode placed over the left sensory-motor cortex (C3 on the 10-20 system). A 90 second video of people walking through a plaza was watched by the clients immediately before and after the Revisioning procedure. Mu (8-12 Hz) relative power was then compared. Decreases in mu (called mu suppression) reflect increases in mirror neuron activity.
>
> The default mode network (DMN) was also monitored with EEG. This electrode monitored activity from the amygdala and prefrontal cortex, between the nasal bridge and the interior edge of the right eyebrow (FPO2). This network should be reduced following

Revisioning as the DMN is hyperactive in depression and trauma.

The first three test instruments are paper/pencil tests that employ a 5-point rating scale. They were administered immediately before the Revisioning procedure and approximately one week later. The first test measures symptoms of complicated grief (persistent complex bereavement disorder). The Mu suppression test gives a direct measure of mirror neuron behavior whereas the Imagery and Empathy scales indirectly measure mirror neuron activities.

If Revisioning produces a decline in complicated grief symptoms, then it can be compared with other treatments and offer sufferers another alternative for relief. The mirror neuron activity could explain why the benefits appear to happen so quickly and persistently.

Results

1. Inventory of Complicated Grief - Grief scores were tabulated on 10 patients. Complicated grief decreased from an average of 24.4 (pre-test) to 19.8 (post-test). A repeated measures t-test value of 3.1 was statistically significant ($p < .003$).

2. Vividness of Visual Imagery - Imagery scores were tabulated on the same 10 patients. Imagery improved following Revisioning by an average of

59.9 to 67.2. A repeated measures t-test value of 1.8 was statistically significant (p < .05).

3. Basic Empathy Scale - Empathy scores were tabulated on the same 10 patients. Empathy scores rose following Revisioning from an average of 69.6 to 79.3. A repeated measures t-test value of 2.0 was statistically significant (p < . 03).

4. EEG - Mu Suppression Test - EEGs were recorded from 5 patients. The Mu suppression test demonstrated that 8-12 Hz activity decreased following Revisioning from an average of 19.0% relative power to 15.0%. A repeated measures t-test value of 1.9 was statistically significant (p < . 05).

5. EEG - FPO2 - EEGs were recorded from 5 patients. Recordings from FPO2 indicated that high beta activity (> 20 Hz; representative of anxiety) decreased significantly from 26.9 to 20.5% relative power. A repeated measures t-test value of 2.4 was statistically significant (p < .03).

Conclusions

Initial clinical research on Revisioning has indicated that this procedure leads to significant improvement within weeks for persistent complex bereavement disorder and other types of unresolved grief.

Furthermore, EEG mu was significantly suppressed following Revisioning, demonstrating that mirror neuron activity was increased. Revisioning also led to significant increases on the Empathy and Imagery Tests. This suggests again that MNN activity is boosted following Revisioning. The fact that mirror neuron change can be facilitated within ten minutes is remarkable in itself.

EEG FPO2 declines indicated that anxiety was significantly abated with Revisioning. This suggests that the default mode activity, considered to represent ruminating, was reduced following Revisioning. This initial research suggests that the mirror neuron network (MNN) is under-functioning in unresolved grief and the default mode network (DMN) is over-functioning.

Just as in phantom limb pain, when the departed person has been re-attached to the mourner, the plasticity of the brain reorganizes itself to re-include the loved one back into the original cortical locations. Evidence now exists that this cortical redistribution can lead to significant recovery from grief.

MIRROR EXPOSURE

Mirror exposure is different from Revisioning but has some interesting applications that may also employ the mirror neuron network. Some of those clinical applications will be covered briefly now. Mirror exposure involves observing oneself in a mirror in order to habituate and restructure negative perceptions of one's body. This has been used successfully with several populations.

Body Dysmorphic Disorder

Mirror exposure has been successful in decreasing negative body image in obese subjects by having them give detailed, neutral descriptions of their bodies to the experimenters (Hilbert, et al., 2002; Jansen, et al., 2008). By focusing on the precise details of their bodies, negative self-appraisals were thereby de-emphasized.

In another study of people with body dysmorphic disorder, the detailed neutral description version of mirror exposure used in the two studies above was compared with two other conditions (Moreno-Dominguez et al., 2012). The second employed mirror exposure without guiding the client through neutral, detailed descriptions, something more akin to implosion therapy. The third condition was an imagery condition control group that did not employ mirror exposure but did have the clients use the guided script along with their mental representations of their bodies. In five 40-minute sessions, there was a significant decrease in body dissatisfaction and negative thoughts in all three groups, with the mirror exposure alone group outperforming only the imagery group at follow-up.

I believe that the improvement in all groups is because the brain's mirror neuron network (MNN) was recruited by the subjects in observing and imagining their bodies. As we've seen with participants of Revisioning, as the MNN activity increases, the default mode network (DMN) then decreases its hyper-functioning as the anxiety and negative ruminations about one's body also decline. Oxytocin, the proposed neuropeptide associated with the MNN, probably plays an important role in helping turn off the DMN.

Oxytocin and the MNN may explain the results of a fascinating study conducted of the National Basketball Association (Kraus et al., 2010). NBA players were coded for how much congratulatory touch was engaged in during just one early season game. The amount of touch was found to be correlated with individual and team performance at the end of the season!

This NBA study corroborates the oxytocin-MNN connection. In this case however, the oxytocin production system was stimulated first through touch, as opposed to Revisioning and mirror exposure where the MNN is recruited first. Could it be that touch produces oxytocin which increases MNN activity which increases visual-motor performance? What a simple formula for all sports and creative arts performance! Can you imagine the symphony orchestra engaging in a group hug before their next performance in order to play at their best?

This seems to be a very important point, that there is a reversible connection between the MNN and the oxytocin/bonding system which is its own reward network, perhaps separate from the pain/reward network involving dopamine.

Mirror Exposure and Childhood Abuse

The mirror neuron network may play a role in causing phantom pain in some patients who exhibit body dysmorphic disorder because of physical and/or sexual childhood abuse. I have seen many patients who have manifested severe pain years later following abuse. The interesting thing is that often the pain has been experienced in body areas which incurred the trauma.

Many victims of abuse whom I have interviewed say they developed patterns of visually or manually "neglecting" body parts where abuse had been suffered. They simply did not want to engage in flashbacks by looking at those body areas so they neglected them instead.

I propose that this process is like phantom limb pain because when the body area is neglected, the sensory-motor cortex reorganizes itself, relegating less cortical space to the body parts avoided.

Research shows that child sexual assault survivors are:

- 2½ times as likely to have pelvic pain and pelvic inflammatory disorder, breast diseases ranging from fibrocystic changes to cancer, and yeast infections;

- 1½ times more bladder infections;

- More likely to have complications of pregnancy and to have chronic pain, including backaches and headaches. The more serious the abuse, the more serious the resulting medical problems (Forrest, 1994).

I have used mirror exposure with childhood abuse survivors who had concurrent pelvic or chest pain and found that body satisfaction improved and pain declined. In these sessions, I used a combined systematic approach using detailed observation of their bodies and cognitive therapy for any body areas that produced negative self-evaluations.

Mirror Exposure in Panic Disorder

Years ago, before biofeedback equipment, I used to teach patients how to do diaphragmatic breathing (to reduce anxiety) by observing themselves in the mirror. What I witnessed was that many patients said they felt relaxed just by looking in the mirror.

Exploring this idea for years in the treatment of anxiety and panic attacks I have found that if someone is on the upslope toward a panic attack, that brief mirror gazing can give people instantaneous positive feedback. "Even though I feel like my insides are going to explode, I look in the mirror and my face looks expressionless and relaxed, my body is not running away like my heart makes me think it is and suddenly I relax." I had a patient who flew on a white-knuckle trip and remembered I had told her about this. She took her phone out and looked at the mirror feature of the camera and began settling down instantly. She even took pictures of herself relaxing along with the white knuckles of the passenger sitting next to her!

I said "upslope" of a panic attack because if you are already in the middle of an attack, your facial expressions may not look so relaxed and the mirror exposure might be counterproductive.

SUMMARY

Revisioning has the ability to produce profound changes in the way we experience grief. One of the important distinctions to make is that this is not just a catharsis-inducing technique. People with persistent complex bereavement may cry quite often, but with no noticeable resolution of their emotions. This is because Revisioning activates the mirror neuron network. It is proposed here that by doing so, the cortical representations of our loved ones reorganizes and causes less emotional pain. If this is true, then stimulating the mirror neuron network has exposed a veritable tip-of-the-iceberg of unexplored theories and techniques for grief in particular, and the whole field of mental health in general. Revisioning and mirror exposure are just two of the many procedures potentially available that stimulate mirror neuron network (MNN) activity in a beneficial direction. The expressive arts therapies can also now be seen to exert their powerful influence via the MNN. Most of the work done in these fields involves imitation, imagination, and empathy.

Revisioning has become such a powerful tool in my practice that I have set up an online service to update practitioners and potential clients alike. This service is DrMarkRider.com/Revisioning.

REFERENCES

American Psychiatric Association. (2013). Diagnostic and statistical manual of mental disorders (5th ed.). Arlington, VA: American Psychiatric Publishing.

Ammaniti M, Lenzi GL. Neurobiological bases of affective mirroring in depressed mother-infant interactions, unpublished scientific report, University of Rome, Department of Neurological Sciences.

Bakermans-Kranenburg MJ, van I Jzendoorn MH. Sniffing around oxytocin: review and meta-analyses of trials in healthy and clinical groups with implications for pharmacotherapy. Trans Psychiatry, 2013 May 21;3.

Baskerville TA, Douglas AJ. Dopamine and oxytocin interactions underlying behaviors: potential contributions to behavioral disorders. CNS Neurosci Ther. 2010 Jun;16(3):e92-123.

Bisconti TL, Bergman CS, Boker SM. Social support as a predictor of variability: An examination of the adjustment trajectories of recent widows. Psychology and Aging, 2006; 21; 3: 590-599.

Bonanno G. The Other Side of Sadness: What the New Science of Bereavement Tells Us About Life After Loss. NY: Basic Books, 2009.

Boucher L. The pregnant homunculus. BrainFacts.org, 2013.

Bowlby, J. Loss: Sadness and Depression. Hogarth, 1980.

Brzezicka A. Integrative deficits in depression and in negative mood states as a result of fronto-parietal network dysfunctions. Acta Neurobiol, 2013;73(3): 313-25.

Bui E, Nadal-Vicens M, Simon NM. Pharmacological approaches to the treatment of complicated grief: rationale and a brief review of the literature. Postgrad Med. 1982 Jul;72(1):172-9.

Burns JW, Quartana PJ, Elfant E, Matsuura J, Gilliam W, Nappi C, Wolff B, Gray E. Shifts in attention biases in response to acute pain induction: examination of a model of "conversion" among repressors. Emotion. 2010 Dec;10(6):755-66.

Cocude M., Charlot V., Denis M. Latency and duration of visual mental images in normal and depressed subjects. Journal of Mental Imagery. 1997;21(1):127–142.

Cornelissen G, Watson D, Mitsutake G, Fiser B, Siegelova J, Dusek J, Vohlidalova M, Svaeinova H, Halberg F. Mapping of circaseptan and circadian changes in mood. Scr Med (Brno). 2005;78(2):89-98.

Crepeau, MT. A comparison of the behavior patterns and meanings of weeping among adult men and women across three health conditions. Dissertation Abstracts Int., 42: 137-8.

de Greck M, Bölter AF, Lehmann L, Ulrich C, Stockum E, Enzi B, Hoffmann T, Tempelmann C, Beutel M, Frommer J, Northoff G. Changes in brain activity of somatoform disorder patients during emotional empathy after multimodal psychodynamic psychotherapy. Front Hum Neurosci. 2013 Aug 16;7:410.

Denollet J, Martens EJ, Nyklicek I, Conraads VM, de Gelder B. Clinical events in coronary patients who report low distress: adverse effect of repressive coping. Health Psychol. 2008 May;27(3):302-8.

Forrest, MS. The relationship of child sexual abuse to medical problems in adulthood. The Healing Woman (Jan. 1994).

Freed PJ, Yanagihara TK, Hirsch J, Mann JJ. Neural mechanisms of grief regulation. Biological Psychiatry, 2009 Jul 1;66(1):33-40

Freud S. Mourning and melancholia. Standard Edition, 1917, 14:243–258.

Freud S. The ego and the id. Standard Edition, 1923, 19:12–66.

Freud S. Five Lectures on Psycho-Analysis. Penguin: 1995: 28-9.

Frey, WH et al. Crying behavior in the human adult. Integrative Psychiatry, 1983, 1:94-100.

Grief<dot>org (2013). Center for Complicated Grief at Columbia University's School of Social Work.

Hendricks L, Bengston W, Gunkleman J. The healing connection: EEG harmonics, entrainment, and Schumann's resonances. Journal of Scientific Exploration, 2010, 24:3, 419-430.

Hilbert, A., Tuschen-Caffier, B., & Vögele, C. Effects of prolonged repeated body image exposure in binge-eating disorder. Journal of Psychosomatic Research, 2002, 52, 137–144.

Holmes TH, Rahe RH. "The Social Readjustment Rating Scale". J Psychosom Res, 1967 11 (2): 213–8.

Huke V, Turk J, Saeidi S, Kent A, Morgan JF. Autism spectrum disorders in eating disorder populations: a systematic review. Eur Eat Disord Rev. 2013 Sep; 21(5):345-51.

Jankowiak-Siuda K, Zajkowski W. A neural model of mechanisms of empathy deficits in narcissism. Med Sci Monit. 2013 Nov 5;19:934-41.

Jansen, A., Bollen, D., Tuschen-Caffier, B., Roefs, A., Tanghe, A., & Braet, C. Mirror exposure reduces body dissatisfaction and anxiety in obese adolescents: A pilot study. Appetite, 2008, 51, 214–217.

Jolliffe D, Farrington, DP. Development and Validation of the Basic Empathy Scale. Journal of Adolescence, v29 n4 p589-611 Aug 2006.

Kleiger RE, Miller, JP, Krone RJ, Bigger JT. The independence of cycle length variability and exercise testing on predicting mortality of patients surviving acute myocardial infarction. Am J Cardiol. 1990 Feb 15;65(7):408-11.

Kraus MW, Huang C, Keltner D. Tactile communication, cooperation, and performance: an ethological study of the NBA. Emotion. 2010 Oct; 10(5):745-9.

Kubler-Ross E. On Death and Dying. NY: Scribner, 1969.

Landin-Romero R, Novo P, Vicens V, McKenna PJ, Santed A, Pomarol-Clotet E, Salgado-Pineda P, Shapiro F, Amann BL. EMDR therapy modulates the default mode network in a subsyndromal, traumatized bipolar patient. Neuropsychobiology. 2013; 67(3): 181-4.

La Cesa S, Tinelli E, Toschi N, Di Stefano G, Collorone S, Aceti A, Francia A, Cruccu G, Truini A, Caramia F. fMRI pain activation in the periaqueductal gray in healthy volunteers during the cold pressor test. Magn Reson Imaging. 2013 Dec 19, S0730-725X(13)00387-1.

Lerner JS, Gonzalez RM, Dahl RE, Hariri AR, Taylor SE. Facial expressions of emotion reveal neuroendocrine and cardiovascular stress responses. Biol Psychiatry. 2005 Nov 1;58(9):743-50.

Marks, D.F. "Visual imagery differences in the recall of pictures". British Journal of Psychology, 1973, 64: 17-24.

McCullough ME, Luna LR, Berry JW, Tabak BA, Bono G. On the form and function of forgiving: modeling the time-forgiveness relationship and testing the valuable relationships hypothesis. Emotion. 2010 Jun;10(3):358-76.

Melson SJ, Rynearson EK. Unresolved bereavement: medical reenactment of a loved one's terminal illness. Dialogues Clinical Neuroscience, 2012 Jun;14(2): 149-57.

Michielsen ME, Selles RW, van der Geest JN, Eckhardt M, Yavuzer G, Stam HJ, Smits M, Ribbers GM, Bussmann JB. Motor recovery and cortical reorganization after mirror therapy in chronic stroke patients. Neurorehabilitation and Neural Repair, 2011, Mar-Apr: 25:223-233.

MirrorBoxTherapy.com

Molnar-Szakacs I, Uddin LQ. Self-Processing and the Default Mode Network: Interactions with the Mirror Neuron System. Front Hum Neurosci, 2013, 7:571.

Moreno-Domíngueza S, Rodríguez-Ruizb S, Fernández-Santaellab C, Jansenc A, Tuschen-Caffier B. Pure versus guided mirror exposure to reduce body dissatisfaction: A preliminary study with university women. Body Image (9) 2012, 285-288.

Norman GJ, Karelina K, Morris JS, Zhang N, Cochran M, Courtney DeVries A. Social interaction prevents the development of depressive-like behavior after post nerve injury in mice: a potential role for oxytocin. Psychosom Med. 2010 Jul;72(6):519-26.

Oberman,LM,Hubbard, EM, McCleery JP, Altschuler, EL, Ramachandran, VS, Pinedad JA. EEG evidence for mirror neuron dysfunction in autism spectrum disorders. Cognitive Brain Research 24, 2005, 190–198.

O'Connor, MF, Wellisch DK, Stanton AL, Eisenberger NI, Irwin MR, Lieberman MD. Craving love? Enduring grief activates the brain's reward center. 2008; Aug. 15; 42(2):969-972.

O'Connor, MF. Dialogues. Immunological and neuroimaging biomarkers of complicated grief: A Review. Clin Neurosci, 2012 Jun;14(2):141-8.

O'Connor MF., Wellisch DK., Stanton AL., Olmstead R., Irwin MR. Diurnal cortisol in complicated and non-complicated grief: Slope differences across the day. Psychoneuroendocrinology. 2012; 37:725–728.

O'Connor MF, Irwin MR, Wellisch DK. When grief heats up: pro-inflammatory cytokines predict regional brain activation. Neuroimage, 2009 Sep;47(3):891-6.

O'Rourke M. Good grief. The New Yorker, Feb. 1, 2010.

Perry A, Bentin S, Shalev I, Israel S, Uzefovsky F, Bar-On D, Ebstein RP. Intranasal oxytocin modulates EEG mu/alpha and beta rhythms during perception of biological motion. Psychoneuroendocrinology. 2010 Nov;35(10):1446-53.

Preston, SD, de Waal FB. Empathy: Its ultimate and proximate bases. Behav Brain Sci. 2002 Feb;25(1): 1-20.

Prigerson HG, Frank E, Kasl SV, Reynolds CF, Anderson B, Zubenko GS, Houck PR, George CJ, Kupfer DJ. Complicated grief and bereavement-related depression as distinct disorders: preliminary empirical validation in elderly bereaved spouses. Am J Psychiatry. 1995 Jan;152(1):22-30.

Prigerson HG, Maciejewski PK, Reynolds CF, Bierhals AJ, Newsom JT, Fasiczka A, Frank E, Doman J, Miller M. Inventory of Complicated Grief: a scale to measure maladaptive symptoms of loss. Psychiatry Res. 1995 Nov 29;59(1-2):65-79.

Quartana PJ, Bounds S, Yoon KL, Goodlin BR, Burns JW. Anger suppression predicts pain, emotional, and cardiovascular responses to the cold pressor. Ann Behav Med. 2010 Jun;39(3):211-21.

Radin, D. (2004). Event-related EEG correlations between isolated human subjects. Journal of Alternative and Complementary Medicine, 10, 315–324.

Ramachandran VS, Hirstein W. The perception of phantom limbs. Brain, 1998, 121, 1603-1630.

Ramachandran VS. The Tell-Tale Brain. 2011: 27, NY: W.W. Norton.

Rider MS, Floyd J, Kirkpatrick J. The effect of music, imagery, and relaxation on adrenal corticosteroids and the re-entrainment of circadian rhythms. J Music Ther. 1985 Spring;22(1):46-58.

Rider MS. The Rhythmic Language of Health and Disease. 1997, Barcelona Press.

Sambataro F, Wolf ND, Pennuto M, Vasic N, Wolf RC. Revisiting default mode network function in major depression: evidence for disrupted subsystem connectivity. Psychol Med. 2013 Oct 31:1-11.

Sbarra DA, Hazan C. Coregulation, dysregulation, self-regulation: an integrative analysis and empirical agenda for understanding adult attachment, separation, loss, and recovery. Pers Soc Psychol Rev. 2008 May;12(2):141-67.

Schippers MB, Roebroeck A, Renken R, Nanetti L, Keysers C. Mapping the information flow from one brain to another during gestural communication. Proc. Natl. Acad. Sci., 2010,107, 9388–9393.

Schreiter S, Pijnenborg GH, Aan HR. Empathy in adults with clinical or subclinical depressive symptoms. J Affective Disorders, 2013 Aug 15;150(1):1-16.

Sephton SE, Lush E, Dedert EA, Floyd AR, Rebholz WN, Dhabhar FS, Spiegel D, Salmon P. Diurnal cortisol rhythm as a predictor of lung cancer survival. Brain Behav Immun. 2013 Mar;30 Suppl:S163-70.

Skrundz M, Bolten M, Nast I, Hellhammer DH, Meinlchmidt G. Plasma oxytocin concentration during pregnancy is associated with development of postpartum depression. Neuropsychopharmacology, 2011 Aug;36(9):1886-93.

Standish, L. J., Johnson, L. C., Richards, T., & Kozak, L. (2003). Evidence of correlated functional MRI signals between distant human brains. Alternative Therapies in Health and Medicine, 9, 122–128.

Standish, L. J., Kozak, L., Johnson, L. C., & Richards, T. (2004). Electroencephaolographic evidence of correlated event-related signals between the brains of spatially and sensory isolated human subjects. Journal of Alternative and Complementary Medicine, 10, 307–314.

Stroebe, Margaret; Stroebe, Wolfgang. Facial expressions of emotion reveal neuroendocrine and cardiovascular stress responses. Journal of Consulting and Clinical Psychology, Vol 59(3), Jun 1991, 479-482.

Wackermann, J., Seiter, C., Keibel, H., & Walach, H. (2003). Correlations between brain electrical activities of two spatially separated human subjects. Neuroscience Letters, 336, 60–64.

Walker J, Lawson R. FPO2 beta training for drug-resistant depression. Journal of Neurotherapy, 2013, 17:198-200.

Wang L, Li K, Zhang QE, Zeng YW, Jin Z, Dai WJ, Su YA, Wang G, Tan YL, Yu X, Si TM. Inter-hemispheric functional connectivity and its relationships with clinical characteristics in major depressive disorder: a resting state fMRI study. PLoS One. 2013;8(3).